Country Music Library

ROBERT K. KRISHEF

Lerner Publications Company ▪ Minneapolis

ACKNOWLEDGMENTS: The photographs are reproduced through the courtesy of: pp. 4, 16, 44, 70, Michael G. Borum; pp. 6, 15, 18, 19, 23, 38, 49, 52, 58, Alanna Nash; pp. 9, 68, Wide World Photos, Inc.; pp. 13, 35, Michael Norcia, Globe Photos, Inc.; pp. 25, 28, 33, 42, 43, 62, Country Music Foundation Library and Media Center, Nashville, Tennessee; p. 45, Sam Trent; p. 55, Warner Brothers Records; p. 56, (left), Charles W. Bush; p. 56 (right), Bonnie Lippel; pp. 61, 66, RCA Records; pp. 65, 68, Katz, Gallin, Morey Enterprises, Inc., © Dolly Parton, Used by Permission.

Front cover photo: Michael G. Borum
Back cover photo: RCA Records

LIBRARY OF CONGRESS CATALOGING IN PUBLICATION DATA

Krishef, Robert K.
  Dolly Parton.

  (Country Music Library)
  Discography: p. 72
  Includes index.
  SUMMARY: Traces the life of Dolly Parton from her child-
hood of poverty in the Great Smoky Mountains to her stardom
as a performer and song writer.

  1. Parton, Dolly—Juvenile literature. 2. Country music—
United States—Biography—Juvenile literature. [1. Parton,
Dolly. 2. Musicians] I. Title.

ML3930.P25K7   784.5'2'00924 [B] [92]   79-28247
ISBN 0-8225-1411-7

Manufactured in the United States of America

International Standard Book Number: 0-8225-1411-7
Library of Congress Catalog Card Number: 79-28247

2 3 4 5 6 7 8 9 10 85 84 83 82 81

Contents

Cinderella 1

Once upon a time, a poor little mountain girl lived in a small shack with her parents and 10 brothers and sisters. They had no running water or electricity or telephone. Rats sometimes scampered across the rickety floor. On winter nights, the shack grew so cold that the children hardly minded sleeping three or four to a bed. They could stay warmer that way.

The little girl and her brothers and sisters always had clothes to wear and food to eat. But the clothes were frequently old and patched. And the food was often only biscuits and gravy and beans and potatoes.

The little girl loved her family deeply, and she was loved just as deeply in return. Still, she couldn't help wishing for a more pleasant life. She wanted to live in a nicer and bigger house, where she could have some privacy. She wanted to look pretty. She wanted to visit places outside the isolated Great Smoky Mountains area of Tennessee, where her family lived.

Dolly wrote "My Tennessee Mountain Home" about this childhood home near Locust Ridge, Tennessee. The Partons lived here for about five years.

Her family had little money and couldn't afford an automobile. So it was difficult to take even short trips to get away for a little while. There never seemed to be any real way for this restless little girl to ever escape. Although there was no real way, there was a magic way. She could use her imagination.

She made believe she was a princess or someone rich and famous. At a very young age, she began to write and sing about those people. In her songs, she "became" the people she wrote about. She would get totally involved in her fantasies. Sometimes she followed butterflies and hummingbirds through the fields, perhaps wishing she, too, could fly away. After following them for a time, she would suddenly realize she had strayed too far from home. Then she would be relieved to hear her mother calling to help her find her way back.

Eventually, of course, the little girl grew up. For most people, growing up would have signaled the end of the fairy-tale life. But for Dolly Rebecca Parton, fantasy has astonishingly turned into truth. Today Dolly Parton is one of the most special and talked-about personalities in show business. Like Cinderella, she leads an exciting life that is remarkably different than her earlier days.

Although she once lived in a mountain shack, she now owns a 23-room mansion. Once she only dreamed of pretty things. Now she has glamorous clothes, beautiful blond wigs, and sparkling diamonds. Instead of living at a near-poverty level, she finds money pouring in from album sales, ownership of music publishing companies, and royalties on sales of Dolly Parton dolls and posters.

The little girl who longed to be famous has been on the cover of *People*, *Life*, *Saturday Evening Post*, and in the centerfold of *Rolling Stone*. She has been written up in the *New York Times* magazine, *Cosmopolitan*, and *TV Guide*. She has been interviewed by Barbara Walters, Johnny Carson, Dinah Shore, and Merv Griffin.

Through exposure from the public media and from more than one thousand personal appearances in the past few years, Dolly has become instantly identifiable by the public. Her obvious physical attraction has not obscured the natural charm and wit that have made her a popular guest on television talk shows. Dolly's talent and determination—along with her appearance, charm, and wit—have turned her childhood fantasies into reality.

Parton is highly respected in the entertainment industry for her dual ability as songwriter and singer. Among hits she has written are "Joshua," "Love Is Like a Butterfly," "Jolene," "The Bargain Store," "My Blue Ridge Mountain Boy," "Coat of Many Colors," "It's All Wrong, But It's All Right," and "Two Doors Down." Her albums "Here You Come Again" and "Heartbreaker" won platinum awards for sales of one million copies, and she is consistently one of RCA's best-selling artists.

Dolly's work has brought scores of honors and trophies from magazines such as *Billboard*, *Record World*, and *Cashbox* and from music industry organizations such as the Academy of Country Music and the Country Music Association. Several times she has been named country music's "Female Vocalist of the Year." Both the Academy of Country Music (in 1977) and the Country Music Association (in 1978) selected her as "Entertainer of the Year."

Dolly Parton—the Academy of Country Music's 1977 "Entertainer of the Year"

Parton has become known as more than a country music star. She has "crossed over" more and more often, which means that her songs and records are hits in the "pop music" category, too. This has happened by design rather than by accident. The backup music of Dolly's band, Gypsy Fever, and the production of her singles and albums are aimed at the huge "middle-of-the-road" audience. Although Dolly's roots are in country music—"And," she says, "I'll always be country"—she wants to be a superstar of the entire entertainment world.

In striving toward this goal with her characteristic determination and ambition, Parton has touched —and has been touched by—the lives of many people. Memories and incidents, as well as people, have influenced and affected her as she has moved, like Cinderella, from one world to another. As she grows and changes professionally, she leaves others behind in their own worlds. Still, in some ways Dolly Parton remains a product of her past, which began on January 19, 1946.

Avie Lee and Robert Lee Parton 2

Avie Lee Owens and Robert Lee Parton came from the so-called hill or mountain people of east Tennessee. Their families settled in the remote valleys, basins, and hillsides of the Great Smoky Mountains, which separate Tennessee from North Carolina. Early occupants of the area were Cherokee Indians. They were later joined by English, Scotch, and Irish immigrants.

Robert Lee and Avie Lee, Dolly Parton's parents, made a handsome and striking couple. Dolly's father had a fair complexion, blue eyes, and light hair. Dolly's mother, part Cherokee, had dark skin, high cheekbones, and black hair. Dolly is a combination of both. She has the fair hair, complexion, and eyes of her father and the dimples, facial features, and smile of her mother.

The couple got married when Robert Lee was 17 and Avie Lee was 15. This was young, even in an area where early marriages were common. But they were bold, determined, and in love. "Mama grew up with us kids," Dolly was to joke years later.

Dolly's parents lived in Sevier County, along the Little Pigeon River of the Great Smokies. Through the years, they lived in a series of shacks or tiny farm homes. Sometimes they were tenant share-croppers, working for another farmer and living on his land. And sometimes they owned their own house. But money was scarce all the time. The Partons were used to a hard life, however, and evidently faced their struggles with great calm.

"Some people may think we were real poor," Avie Lee says today. "But I can't see it that way. We were just ordinary Americans, and I was always real proud of what we had."

Robert Lee, or Lee, as he was generally called, was the family's provider. He raised tobacco as a cash crop and beans, potatoes, corn, and turnips for food. He also did construction work, dug ditches, worked occasionally on jobs with government proj-ects, and made moonshine whiskey—which was an accepted activity in the mountains even though it was illegal. Avie Lee, meanwhile, raised the family, which grew quickly and steadily.

The Partons' first child, Willadeene, was born about a year after they got married. Then came David and Denver. Dolly, their fourth child, was born on January 19, 1946, when Avie Lee was 22 years old. Willadeene, who was only about 6 years old at the time, recalls people coming "from miles around to see our beautiful new baby."

Today Robert and Avie Lee Parton live on a farm 30 miles from Nashville.

After Dolly, there came Bobby, Stella, Cassie, Randy, Larry, Floyd and Frieda, who were twins, and Rachel, the youngest. Larry lived only a few hours. The Parton children felt their brother's loss,

Dolly was about ten years old when the Partons moved to this small farm near Caton's Chapel, Tennessee.

however, as deeply as if they had known him well. The older ones who were acquainted with the tragedy still refer to themselves as a family of 12 brothers and sisters. Dolly's biographies read that way, too. But there were really only 11 children in the Parton household.

With 11 children, it seemed that Avie Lee was always pregnant with one child and holding another in her arms. She also was ill much of the time. In the Parton household, therefore, as in other large families, the older children had to help care for the younger ones. Willadeene, Dolly, and Stella were like substitute mothers. After Dolly became successful in show business, she was often quoted as saying she felt as if she had been raising children all her life. Even after she got her own home, younger brothers, sisters, and relatives frequently spent time living with her.

Although the Parton children talk about the good moments of growing up, they also feel twinges of pain when they remember some of their childhood experiences. It was true that many other families did not have much more than the Partons did. But few families had as little. There often was no money for a doctor when Avie Lee was ill. There was rarely any meat to eat. About once a year, Lee Parton slaughtered a hog, but it didn't last long with so many people to feed. Even the outside of the house was depressing. "We didn't have any grass," said Dolly. "Mama used to sweep out the yard."

Yet Avie Lee and Lee Parton had enough character and determination to keep their family going through bitter struggles and periods of discouragement. Dolly and her brothers and sisters look back with love and respect at the way their parents held the family together. Dolly says firmly about her father, "He's the smartest man I've ever known." She is referring to his common sense and native shrewdness, since he could neither read nor write.

Dolly with her father—
"the smartest man I've ever known"

Besides being smart, Lee Parton was the disciplinarian of the household. He established firm codes of behavior that his older daughters in particular considered too strict and old-fashioned. For example, they fussed about a rule that did not allow them to wear makeup. Dolly, who dreamed as a child about using lipstick, found a way to rebel against the rule. She put Merthiolate—a red solution used to cleanse cuts—on her lips. It stung briefly, but "Daddy could never rub *that* off," she said, grinning.

Avie Lee Parton was easier on the children. This might have been because she was often too ill to be a disciplinarian, or because she remembered growing up herself under overly strict supervision. Dolly thinks that, in a sense, her mother was rebelling along with her children. The first thing Avie Lee did after she got married was to cut her long, black hair. Her father had never allowed her to cut it.

Avie Lee's father, the Reverend Jake Owens, preached fiery sermons at the little church the Partons attended. Gospel singing was an important part of the prayer and revival meetings. The sermons and songs about the power and wrath of God, and the joy of accepting Him, left a permanent impression on Dolly.

Dolly began singing in church at the age of six, first with the congregation and later by herself. From the very beginning, she was excited by the emotion and drive of the old country spirituals and hymns. "I think that the soul feeling I get in my voice started with my church-singing days," she said. "The same feeling and sincerity leaks

The Reverend Jake Owens, Dolly's grandfather, in the pulpit of his church near Sevierville

over into anything I sing now." Many of the songs she later wrote had a gospel flavor. One of them, "Daddy Was an Old Time Preacher Man," was inspired by Reverend Owens.

Singalongs were an important element of home life, too. The Partons had no television. There were few, if any, newspapers or books to read. And the radio worked only if someone could find batteries. So everyone looked forward to the singing sessions, in which both Avie Lee and Lee participated. They both came from musical families. Avie Lee knew many folk ballads and even composed her own. Lee accompanied the sessions on guitar and banjo.

No one enjoyed the singalongs more than Dolly. Actually, she didn't need to be in a group to sing. Her parents recall that she started singing to herself almost before she could talk. "She would carry a tune before she could say the words," explained Avie Lee. "And before she was a year and one-half, she could sing a little rhyme or song."

By the time she was five, Dolly was creating her own rhymes. Her mother remembers the thrill of the first time Dolly came to her and said, "Mama,

The sign above the door of Owen's church reads, "House of Prayer for All People, Isa. (Isaiah) 56:7."

I've made a song." Avie Lee still has the first song she wrote down for her now-famous daughter. It is, as one can imagine, a family keepsake.

Dolly's progress continued. At the age of seven, she made a "guitar" from an old mandolin and two guitar strings. Later, her Uncle Bill Owens gave her a real guitar. She kept composing songs and singing everywhere, all the time—whether working around the farm, washing dishes, taking care of her younger brothers and sisters, or chasing butter-flies in the fields.

It probably was Dolly's way of escaping from some of the harsh reality around her. Avie Lee noticed these flights into fantasy. But she encour-aged her young daughter's dreams then and later. "Mama never let us lose our hopes," said Dolly.

So when the opportunity came to do something about those hopes and dreams, 10-year-old Dolly Parton was ready.

Bill Owens 3

When the mountain folks of Sevier County could get their battery radios working, they enjoyed listening to country music. The Grand Ole Opry was the most popular program in the area. It was broadcast by radio station WSM in Nashville, Tennessee, and had a nationwide audience.

But there were also many programs and stations with strong regional audiences. One such station was WIVK in Knoxville, Tennessee, about 40 miles southeast of the Sevier county seat of Sevierville. The Knoxville area was known for its dams, the University of Tennessee, and other famous institutions and sights. But to country music folks, the best-known institution in Knoxville was a man named Cas Walker.

Walker was a supermarket tycoon, a politician, and an occasional country music performer. He was on WIVK radio and television throughout the day. He would report the news, chat, advertise his supermarkets and various activities, and present entertainment by local musicians. One of his most successful programs was "The Farm and Home Hour."

Among the thousands of listeners and admirers of Cas Walker's shows was Dolly's uncle, Bill Owens, the brother of Dolly's mother. Like others in his family, Bill Owens was musically inclined. Unlike most of them, however, he was interested in a career in show business as a professional writer or performer. Since he was so aware of country music as a money-making field, he began to think about the possibilities that might open up for his young niece.

"I heard her singing many times," he said. "And she was good. The thought came to me that I should take her to the Cas Walker broadcasts."

The true role Bill Owens played in shaping Dolly Parton's professional life is uncertain. At one time, he was credited with being an extremely significant influence on her. "He believed in me," Dolly remarked. "He was responsible for everything I did in the early part of my career." She added that her success "might have happened anyway, but there's a chance it might not have happened if it hadn't been for him."

Recent articles and books about Parton, though, have downgraded Owens' role. They question his talent and picture him as possibly doing more harm than good or as "riding on her coattails," meaning that he used his niece for his benefit as well as for her own. Some of Dolly's current publicity does not even mention him by name. Instead, she refers to him as "my uncle" or "an uncle."

Cas Walker

Whatever Bill Owens' influence was, however, there can be little doubt about his presence and contributions at certain vital times. He encouraged Dolly's singing when she was a youngster. He worked with her on songwriting. And he rehearsed with her for an audition with the Cas Walker show and brought her there.

The audition took place when Dolly was 10 years old. News spread quickly throughout the station about the "talented young kid" trying out for the show. "Announcers and other people from all over the building came in to listen," recalled Owens. "Cas Walker hired Dolly right on the spot."

Eventually, Dolly became a regular performer with Walker, singing during vacation breaks from school. She earned $20 a week, which was a significant sum. Willadeene and other children who worked in the school cafeteria, for example, considered themselves lucky to make $1 a week.

Dolly must have been thrilled to get money for doing what she did so naturally. Sometime during this period, she began to think seriously of a professional career. She talked about being on the Grand Ole Opry. For most mountain folks, such talk was as unrealistic as a fairy tale. Children and adults laughed at her. But Dolly's mother and her Uncle Bill, among others, encouraged her.

Soon Dolly cut her first record. Together, she and Owens had written the song called, "Puppy

Love." She recorded it for Gold Band Records, a small company in Lake Charles, Louisiana. Although the record didn't sell well, "It was a start," said Dolly. "We had big dreams."

One of her big dreams came true when she was 13. She sang on the Grand Ole Opry, thanks to the combination of persistence and a fortunate break. Bill Owens had borrowed a car to take Dolly to Nashville. He tried to get her on the Opry. But that was impossible, they were told, because she was too young.

From 1941 to 1974, the Grand Ole Opry was broadcast from Nashville's Ryman Auditorium.

They didn't take no for an answer, however. While the Opry was on, they talked backstage with officials and performers. Finally, one of the performers Dolly was pestering, Jimmy C. Newman, smiled and said she could take his turn on stage.

Dolly realized that her family and relatives were listening back home, "just in case." She was thoroughly excited but showed remarkable poise. She sang two songs and several encores to thunderous applause. For the first time, young Dolly Parton knew what it felt like to be a star.

Of course, a number of years passed between that incident and actual stardom. But the goal was becoming clearer. When Bill Owens had a car, he and Dolly made more trips to Nashville. They would sleep in the car, wash up in filling station rest rooms, and then make the rounds of record companies and song publishers with Dolly's demonstration tapes.

By the time Dolly entered high school, she had blossomed out both physically and as a performer. Her figure had reached the proportions that it is today. She looked physically mature for her years, and she was much more mature than most of her classmates in ambition and determination. Her voice had developed a special sound that combined childlike tenderness with adult passion and emotion. She could make a high, sometimes trembling sound that was stirring and effective.

Dolly continued to write more songs, to make more demonstration tapes, and to appear on Cas Walker's shows and elsewhere. Her salary with Walker reached $60 a week before she graduated from high school. Dolly's efforts in Nashville also paid off in a limited way. She recorded "It's Sure Gonna Hurt" for Mercury Records and got a songwriting contract with Tree Publishing Company. Neither the record nor her efforts with Tree Publishing were particularly successful, but she was gaining valuable experience.

Meanwhile, Dolly was drifting through high school. She didn't like school, and she didn't have many friends, possibly because she had little in common with other students. Her interest was music, not books. Formal education never had a high priority in the Parton household. Dolly's father had no education. He did not feel it was important for her to stay in school, and her mother agreed. Many people would have dropped out of school under such circumstances, yet Dolly did not. Her staying in school was an example of her determination. She wanted to prove to herself she could get her diploma, and thus she became the first member of her family to finish high school.

For several years, Dolly had not talked much publicly about her professional ambitions because she had gotten tired of being ridiculed. But her plans hadn't changed. A few weeks before high school graduation, Bill Owens had moved to Nashville with his wife and young son and rented a house. "I felt that Dolly was too young to be turned loose alone in a city the size of Nashville," her mother said.

On graduation day, Dolly looked people squarely in the eye, as if daring them to laugh. While other graduates were expressing modest hopes for the future, she declared that she was going to Nashville to become a country music star. The next day she boarded the bus to seek her fortune.

In 1970 Dolly returned to her hometown for "Dolly Parton Day."

Carl Dean   4

It was June 1964, and Carl Dean was 21 years old. In a few months, he would go into the army. Now, though, he was enjoying his idle time driving around in his white, 1963 Chevrolet. He attracted much attention in the sparkling clean, smoothly running car.

On one of his casual excursions through the streets of Nashville, Carl saw an attractive blonde girl. She was walking with a bouncy, lighthearted step, looking at everything with animated interest. He honked, waved, and hollered a greeting. To his surprise, the young girl smiled and waved back. So he pulled over to the curb, and the two began talking.

The girl was Dolly Parton. She had arrived in Nashville that very day, carrying a cardboard suitcase full of original songs and dirty clothes. She had left Sevierville so fast after graduating from high school that she had no time to wash her clothes. After putting her clothes in a washing machine at a laundromat, she had decided to take a walk and see the sights.

For as long as she could remember, Dolly had been naturally optimistic. She believed that if she thought about something hard enough and worked for it hard enough, it would come true. Still, in spite of her cheery nature, Dolly found that being in Nashville was a little frightening. Although she wasn't a complete stranger to the town, she certainly didn't feel at home there, either. It had almost been a relief when the lanky, good-looking young man said hello to her.

Carl was immediately enchanted by this attractive girl. She was not only nice-looking, but also had a pleasant personality, and he felt comfortable with her. Quickly, he asked her to go for a ride. In spite of Dolly's country friendliness, she wouldn't get into a car or go on a date with someone she didn't know. But she said he could call on her the next day at her uncle's house, where she was staying.

Back at the laundromat, they continued to talk while Dolly gathered her clothes. Then Carl drove off, her address in hand, feeling eager and elated about seeing her again.

For a week, the two met every day while Dolly baby-sat with her young nephew. Her uncle, Bill Owens, was performing as a musician out of town. Her aunt, Cathy, was working as a waitress. Since no one else was home, Dolly wouldn't let Carl in the house. So they sat and talked on the front porch.

Then Cathy had a day off. For the first time, Carl and Dolly went out together. He took her home to meet his parents.

Carl knew that he was rapidly falling in love. Dolly was, too. But while he was happy, she was troubled. After all, she had come to Nashville to pursue a career in country music. Marriage was not part of her plans.

Soon Carl left for the army. For a while, there was no need to make a decision about getting married. Dolly moved into her own apartment and concentrated on her career. It was a struggle. She and her Uncle Bill—when he was in town— pounded on door after door, trying to arrange auditions for her. Owens knew some people through his work as a musician. But as far as promotion was concerned, "He didn't know his way around the business any better than I did," said Dolly.

For a few weeks, her meals consisted mainly of mustard and hot dog relish. Dolly had to work part-time as a waitress to supplement her income from occasional singing jobs. Finally, she got an interview with Fred Foster of Monument Records and Combine Publishing Company.

Foster thought that Parton showed promise. Her makeup and her singing mannerisms were clearly unsophisticated. But she had a fresh, winning appearance and a distinctive voice that impressed him. Also, he liked some of the material Dolly had written or had co-written with Bill Owens. He signed them as a songwriting team for Combine and signed Dolly to a recording contract with Monument. She was paid $50 a week as a "draw," or advance against writing or recording royalties.

Ironically, Monument Records first tried to record Dolly as a pop or light rock singer. "I guess they figured my voice was so weird that country people would never go for it," she said. Or perhaps Monument was ahead of its time in defining her proper musical role, since today Dolly is a singer of pop as well as country tunes. But she wasn't ready for such a role in the mid-1960s. "I just didn't fit in with rock crowds and never enjoyed the music at all," she said.

The period at Monument was not a waste, however. Dolly was learning how to look and dress like a star. She was also learning how to make "demos" (demonstration records) that might persuade record companies to buy the songs she had written.

One of the demos was a tune called, "Put It Off until Tomorrow," which she had written with her Uncle Bill Owens. Her uncle took it to a friend, country singer Bill Phillips. Phillips took it to his producer at Decca (now MCA) Records, Owen Bradley. Bradley agreed to produce the record if he could use the woman who had sung harmony on the demo. That woman was Dolly Parton.

She got permission from Monument, and "Put It Off until Tomorrow" became a Bill Phillips hit on the country music charts. Although Dolly's name wasn't on the record, her voice helped make it a hit. Monument Records was then convinced to try her as a country artist.

Dolly's first release for Monument was "Dumb Blonde," a song written by Curly Putnam. Her second was her own song, "Something Fishy." Both records became country music hits. With these successes, plus her increasing recognition as a songwriter, Dolly was now considered a rising young artist.

Meanwhile, the time had come to make a decision about marriage. Carl Dean had returned home. They had talked. Dolly stressed that, while she loved him, she would not marry him unless they understood each other. Nothing could interfere with her music and her determination to be a star.

Dean agreed. "If that's what will make you happy," he said, "that's the way it will be." They were married on May 30, 1966. Since then, Dolly has become one of the biggest names in show business. And her relationship with Dean has grown stronger over the years. Sometimes people in the entertainment business don't believe this. This is because most of them have never seen Dean. Some people used to joke that he "was just a figment of Dolly Parton's imagination."

The 23-room Dean mansion outside of Nashville was built in 1973.

It has become clear through the years, though, why Dean was able to agree not to interfere with his wife's music or her business life. He wants nothing to do with that sort of world. A quiet, reserved man, Dean does not enjoy mingling with strangers and is uncomfortable at public functions. Although he occasionally joins Dolly on the road, he prefers to stay at home.

By profession, he is an asphalt contractor. He paves just enough driveways in Nashville to keep himself as busy as he wants to be. He is also a natural handyman, and he likes to tinker with machinery and work around the house. He and one of Dolly's uncles built the 23-room house in which he and Dolly now live.

Dolly has said that she "doesn't depend on any man for strength." This is true as far as her career is concerned. But she would be the first to agree that the "man in her life"—her husband—has helped her career in another way. Although the relationship has given her the freedom to do what she wants, Dean provides the solid stability she needs when she stops traveling and wants to relax in privacy.

Dean reminds Dolly of her father. He is independent, honest, moral, and unselfish. In fact, she even calls him "Daddy." "He's a home-based type of person and is different from me," she said. "But he's very deep and witty and he's good for me. There's nobody else like him, and I know in my heart that there will never be another person for me."

Porter Wagoner 5

Although Dolly Parton and Carl Dean have had a happy relationship, Dolly would never give up her career for her marriage. It is ironic, therefore, that her big break resulted from another singer's giving up her career for her marriage.

That singer was a woman named Norma Jean, who performed with long-time country music star Porter Wagoner. In 1960 Wagoner hired Norma Jean for his new syndicated television show. She had had some success as a vocalist with the Red Foley "Ozark Jubilee" television show in Springfield, Missouri. But it was the exposure she had on Wagoner's show that made her one of the better known female faces in country music.

By 1967 Wagoner's syndicated show had been seen in 80 cities by an estimated 40 million people. And Norma Jean had made numerous hit records first for Columbia and then for RCA in the early and middle 1960s. Her popularity probably would have continued to grow had she chosen to remain with Wagoner. Instead, she left his show in 1967 to get married and move to Oklahoma.

Porter Wagoner

Porter immediately started looking for another female singer with the right "chemistry"—one who would fit the format and appeal of both his road show and his television program. He interviewed and auditioned newcomers as well as established performers. Many of them had talent, but they didn't meet Wagoner's specific needs or standards. Then he called Dolly Parton.

The two had never met, and Porter hadn't even seen her perform. But he had heard about her and was familiar with her two Monument records, "Dumb Blonde" and "Something Fishy." "I thought that she had potential," he said, "and that she was searching for the right way to be recorded."

Another consideration was Dolly's writing ability. In the past, she had submitted some songs to Wagoner for possible recording by Norma Jean. Although Porter ultimately decided that the material wasn't right for Norma Jean, he still thought that it was well written. So it certainly must have occurred to him that Dolly could provide original songs for his show.

When Dolly received Wagoner's call, she couldn't be sure whether he was interested in her or in her songs. She hoped it was her, because Norma Jean's job was one of the most sought-after in the industry.

Parton brought her guitar to the audition. After she and Wagoner talked for a while, she sang some of her songs for him. Wagoner was quite impressed.

"She was a beautiful girl and sang well," he said. "But the deciding factor was her warmth and sincerity. She had the type of genuine, likable personality that I could sell to people on television and in person." It didn't take him long to offer her a job. And Dolly jumped at the chance to accept.

Since Dolly's contract with Monument Records and Combine Publishing was about to expire, Wagoner wanted her to join him at RCA Records. He had been recording there for about 20 years. "She would be with a company where I had prestige, where I knew the operation, and where I could help her best," he explained.

But some people were not as convinced as Wagoner about Parton's singing ability. One of the doubters was famous guitarist Chet Atkins, who was also an executive and expert analyzer of talent for RCA. Atkins wasn't interested in signing Dolly. "She can't sing," he told Wagoner.

Wagoner was just as positive that she *could* sing. He told Atkins that if RCA lost any money on Dolly's records, the company could "take it out of my royalties." He never had to make good on his offer. The first record Dolly cut for RCA, "Just Because I'm a Woman," sold 150,000 copies and was number one on the country music charts.

"They've never lost a dime on me," said Parton, who has been kidding Atkins ever since about his mistaken judgment.

After joining Wagoner, Dolly had to prove herself in person as well as on record. This was even more difficult than convincing Atkins. Country fans had liked Norma Jean. Dolly was, in her own words, stepping into "big, big shoes." She was prepared for the fact that some fans would resent her. The first few weeks were "torture" for Dolly. When she would start to sing, people would begin calling for Norma Jean. Wagoner recalls that he knew Dolly "had the backbone to stand up to this." Until people got used to her, however, the pressure was almost as hard on him as it was on her. Then he thought of a way to ease the pressure, reassure Dolly, and help them get better acquainted. They started singing together on the bus while traveling.

To Wagoner's surprise, their voices blended as if they had been harmonizing with each other all their lives. He had always been basically a solo performer and had certainly never intended to share the spotlight equally with Dolly Parton when he hired her. But he recognized that they together could offer a new dimension in entertainment. The informal practice sessions on the bus were initially for fun and to build Dolly's confidence. Before long, however, they took on a more serious, professional nature. Within a few weeks, the sessions moved from the bus to the recording studio.

In October 1967, Dolly and Porter recorded their first duet single, "The Last Thing on My Mind."

This was quickly followed in January 1968 by "Holding On to Nothin'," and in the next few years by such other hits as "We'll Get Ahead Someday," "Just Someone I Used to Know," "The Pain of Loving You," "Run That by Me One More Time," and "Daddy Was an Old Time Preacher Man."

In 1968 Parton and Wagoner won the "Vocal Group of the Year" award from the Country Music Association (CMA). They were CMA's "Vocal Duo of the Year" in 1970 and 1971. Norma Jean was

Porter and Dolly (third and fourth from left) *pose with other winners at the 1968 Country Music Association Awards. Those who received awards included Johnny Cash* (left), *Tammy Wynette* (fourth from right), *and Glen Campbell* (third from right).

"Dolly Parton Day" in Sevierville, 1970

forgotten, and Dolly Parton had become a featured performer in her own right. She was establishing an increasingly large following as she sang solo and together with Wagoner on his syndicated television show and in his road show. In 1969 Dolly joined the Grand Ole Opry—another dream come true—which further added to her stature. By the early 1970s, Porter Wagoner and Dolly Parton had become inseparable in the minds of country music fans. If somebody mentioned one, people thought

of the other one right away. Some fans even thought the two were married.

Dolly matured in several ways during the years she spent with Wagoner. Her grooming as a performer, which Fred Foster started at Monument Records, continued under the supervision of Wagoner. It was during this period that she developed a glamorous image and became known for her collection of wigs, sparkling clothes, and jewelry. She learned, too, how to project her personality to catch the mood of the audience and how to work the crowd.

Parton freely gives Wagoner considerable credit for the lessons she learned from him. She does not feel that "he made me a star." But she knows that being with him gave her the opportunity to be a star, and she has always acknowledged his creativity, showmanship, and business sense.

The experience helped Dolly's songwriting as well. Her success as a performer gave her fresh confidence, incentive, and energy to write some of the most memorable songs of her career. The material for these songs was readily available. All Dolly had to do was to remember her childhood.

Joseph   6

When Dolly Parton was a child, she loved to listen to her mother sing and tell stories from the Bible. One of her favorite stories came from the Old Testament. It was about Joseph and his special coat: "Now Israel loved Joseph more than all his children, because he was the son of his old age; and he made him a coat of many colors" (Genesis 37:3). "I used to cry when Mama got to the part when Joseph's brothers sold him into Egypt," said Dolly.

But it was the colorful coat that fascinated her the most. She could imagine how excited Joseph must have been when he received it. When Dolly was about eight years old, she was thrilled to find what her mother was doing at the old pedal sewing machine. Avie Lee had rummaged around in her box of material scraps and had found patches of green, blue, red, and yellow corduroy to make a coat of many colors for Dolly.

The coat was finished in time for Dolly to wear to school on picture-taking day. But the child's pride and anticipation quickly turned to despair and humiliation. Although she felt she was wearing a pretty coat "that came from the Bible," other children laughed at it. They teased Dolly. They tried to tear the coat off, which made her even more embarrassed because she did not have a blouse on underneath. Then they locked her in a pitch-black closet and left her there screaming.

The incident hurt Dolly deeply. For years, even after she grew up, she couldn't talk about it. Finally, she was able to tell about it in a song, "Coat of Many Colors." In the words to the song and in the way she sang them, Dolly stirringly conveyed her heartfelt emotion about the coat "my mama made for me." The song became a country music classic in the late 1960s, and achieved pop music recognition as well.

This song is typical of the way Parton relives her childhood. She pours out her feelings in making music the way some people do in talking to psychiatrists. "I get things out of my system by writing about them," she says. But this has not always completely worked. For example, Dolly still cannot go to sleep without a light on in the room because of the closet incident, perhaps, or the memory of rats scampering around her family's shack at night, or for other reasons. In both her

professional and private life, however, she is considered as well adjusted as anyone in show business. Dolly agrees. "My life is in good order," she says. "I listen to myself and follow my own dreams."

In her writing, as in her singing, Parton is a sensitive communicator. She is a student of people. On stage she can respond to a glancing smile or a shifting mood. Her lyrics tell musical stories that affect her listeners' innermost thoughts and feelings. Although Dolly greatly enjoys singing, "I could live without it if I had to," she remarked. "But I don't think I could live without being able to write. Writing is awfully personal to me."

Her stories paint realistic word-pictures, enhanced by the tunes forever running through her mind. Even her fantasies have an element of reality. She says she has a "wild imagination," but she usually relates her ideas to people, places, or events. There seems to be no end to her memories of life in the Great Smoky Mountains. In a spurt of creativity, Dolly can write as many as 20 songs in one day. Approximately 500 of her songs have been published, but she says that she has "thousands more" on paper or in her head. "If I never wrote anything else, I couldn't live long enough to publish everything I have now," she has stated.

Sometimes getting a song out of her system can be painful. She often writes about unhappy experiences such as the one in "Coat of Many Colors," or the death of a child as in "Me and Little Andy" and "Jeannie's Afraid of the Dark," or going to bed hungry as in "In the Good Old Days (When Times Were Bad)." She doesn't apologize for dwelling on such subjects. "Life isn't all a dance," was her reply to a comment about "Me and Little Andy."

Yet Parton is not a cynic who finds fault with life. She is, rather, a person who experiences and creates many moods: the love that makes the world "a better place to live"; the peacefulness of her Tennessee mountain home; the nostalgia of "remembering Mama and Daddy."

The songs she creates are equally varied. They can be spiritual or religious in nature ("Seeker," "God's Coloring Book"), or hard-driving folk ("Joshua," "Jolene"), or mellow pop ("I Will Always Love You," "Love Is Like a Butterfly"), or rock ("All I Can Do"). In her "Heartbreaker" album, released in 1978, there was even a disco sound in "Baby I'm Burning" and "Sure Thing."

By crossing over musical boundaries, Dolly is demonstrating her refusal to be known as a performer or writer of only a certain type of music. She wants to show her versatility as an artist. And indeed she does astound many reviewers and critics with her ability to change musical beats without losing her rapport and appeal.

Parton is like the eagle of her song, "Light of a Clear Blue Morning." That song starts simply with piano and voice, moves into a faster tempo and a country flavor, and ends with a set of rock-and-gospel choruses. Symbolically, the lyrics state that Dolly has won her artistic independence and is free "to fly as high as her wings can carry her."

In a sense, she has been fighting for such independence all her life. But to most observers, the struggle really began when she left Porter Wagoner's show in 1974.

Emmylou Harris and Dolly backstage at the Grand Ole Opry

Emmylou Harris and Linda Ronstadt 7

Shock waves rippled across the country music public when Dolly Parton left Porter Wagoner's show. Fans felt as though a couple very close to them had been divorced. Of course, Wagoner and Dolly were not married to each other. But they seemed like a couple because they were together so much in public and because of the nature of the songs they sang together.

Reporters and critics have written a great deal about the split between the two performers, which makes it seem complicated. In reviewing Dolly's development, however, the reason for the split seems simple. "You have to follow your own dreams," Parton has stated. Her dream was to be a superstar, and she couldn't be one while working for someone else.

By 1974 Dolly was earning about $60,000 a year with Wagoner. That sum would have seemed like a fortune to her a decade earlier. But Dolly was no longer the unsophisticated high school graduate she was when she boarded the bus to Nashville.

She knew what superstars could earn. Why should she be satisfied earning thousands of dollars, she felt, when she could be making hundreds of thousands of dollars?

Apart from the money, however, Dolly needed to assert her own personality and creativity. Her roots were in country music, but her tastes were not restricted to one musical category. She used to say that she would always be country, but she never declared that she would be willing to remain *only* country.

Moreover, Parton was not alone in her philosophy. There was a growing trend toward the so-called new breed of performer, the performers who believed that labels were not necessary. Just be yourself, they stated. Emmylou Harris and Linda Ronstadt, who were friends and admirers of Dolly, were greatly respected by Dolly as two of the important singers who were carving out their own distinct musical identities.

Harris had started her career as a folk singer. When she made hit albums such as "Pieces of the Sky" and "Elite Hotel" in the early and middle 1970s, her sound gradually eased into a combination of country and hard rock. When asked to describe her vocals, she would simply shrug and say, "I'm not a trained singer. I just sing what I feel."

In 1974 Ronstadt began a string of platinum award-winning albums that included "Heart Like a

Emmylou Harris

Wheel," "Prisoner in Disguise," "Hasten Down the Wind," "Linda Ronstadt's Greatest Hits," and "Living in the U.S.A." In the opinion of many people, among them Dolly Parton, Ronstadt has one of the greatest female voices of all time. Ronstadt draws her fans from a cross-section of musical audiences.

Olivia Newton-John

Linda Ronstadt

It was considered a compliment to Dolly's writing ability when her songs were recorded by outstanding performers like Ronstadt and Harris. Ronstadt released "I Will Always Love You," while Harris did "Coat of Many Colors." Other rock and pop singers, such as Olivia Newton-John and Maria Muldaur, also recorded songs written by Parton. Such recognition by people outside her own immediate musical world helped to open Dolly's eyes further—especially when she was already restless about her career.

Thus there must have been a clash of wills and personalities in the recording studio between the evolving new star, Dolly Parton, and the traditional country music star, Porter Wagoner. It was inevitable that she would leave Wagoner in her search for individuality, just as it was inevitable earlier that she would leave Fred Foster and Monument Records when she had a chance to better herself with Wagoner.

Wagoner was far from pleased with Parton's action. He was, after all, a long-time star who was about to be overshadowed by his pupil. Moreover, he had devoted much of his recent career to grooming Dolly and sharing the spotlight with her. Leaving him might have been a natural step for her, but to Wagoner it seemed to show a lack of gratitude.

Nevertheless, immediately following their breakup, Dolly and Wagoner were represented in publicity as "still being friends." Indeed, they did continue to operate their publishing company and other businesses together, and Wagoner still produced her records. Meanwhile, Parton organized her own road show backed by the new "Traveling Family Band," which consisted mainly of her relatives. She also became the star of her own syndicated television show, "Dolly." The show was produced by Bill Graham of Show Biz, the company that also produced Porter Wagoner's television program.

For the next two years or so, Dolly was extremely busy. Yet she felt that she was "spinning her wheels" as far as her career was concerned. She wasn't making the progress that she had anticipated.

She was heavily booked into one-night performances across the country. But she was dissatisfied with the people managing her bookings. Also, her backup band was not providing the sound she wanted.

Her television show was something of a disappointment as well. Dolly was not happy with its quality. "The show wasn't me," she remarked. One of the few programs she was comfortable with was the show that featured Emmylou Harris and Linda Ronstadt as guest stars. After taping 26 shows, she stopped production.

By mid-1976, Parton was tired. Her vocal cords were giving her trouble. Tension was developing in her relationship with Porter Wagoner. She needed a rest, and she needed to think things over. She cancelled about 65 bookings, worth approximately $325,000, and went into seclusion. Then she found the strength to make the changes she believed she had to make. "The joy of living is just doing what you really want to do," she was to say later.

The decisions she reached, which were carried out early in 1977, shook the entertainment business. Previously, Dolly had left Porter Wagoner's show to go off on her own. Even in their shock, fans of the duo could understand that desire. Now, however, it appeared that she was leaving the country music industry.

Parton completely broke away from all business ventures with Wagoner. Her album "All I Can Do," released in 1976, was the last album he would produce for her. From now on, Dolly would be her own producer, or she would hire someone to steer her in what she thought was the proper creative direction.

Dolly broke up her band ("fired her relatives" was the outcry from some observers) and formed a new one, Gypsy Fever. It was composed of "more versatile and qualified" musicians, who were not necessarily from Nashville. She also moved the base of her business operations from Nashville to Los Angeles, where she signed with the management firm of Katz, Gallin and Cleary. This was the firm that managed such other "crossover" stars as Mac Davis, Olivia Newton-John, and Marie and Donny Osmond. And finally, she recorded her albums in Los Angeles instead of in Nashville.

Now Dolly was in a vastly different artistic and business atmosphere, an atmosphere designed for pop or rock performers such as Linda Ronstadt, rather than country stars like Porter Wagoner. There was a furious reaction from some country music traditionalists. They charged Parton with "going Hollywood," and "turning her back on her people."

Dolly was hurt and angered by the criticism. But she displayed the same backbone as she did years earlier, when people were calling for Norma Jean. "I guess I'm really a pretty brave little number," she remarked.

To her critics, she responded that "I'm still the same Dolly Parton. I'm not leaving country. I'm taking it with me." In her view, she could still be—and was—loyal to Nashville, to her roots, to her memories. But she believed that she owed herself another loyalty, too. And that was to her future.

Composer-singer Eddie Rabbitt toured with Dolly in 1978.

Dolly Parton 8

In 1977 and 1978, the controversy about Dolly Parton gradually simmered down. Some people still resented her decisions. But the passage of time started to heal the wounds, and her fans began to accept what Dolly was trying to do. And, from a financial standpoint, it was clear that she had helped—not hurt—her career.

Her record sales were greater than ever, because she was now a crossover artist. Her audience included the pop, rock, and middle-of-the-road markets in addition to country music fans. She had signed a contract to do three films for Twentieth Century Fox. She had performed on the "Royal Jubilee" television special in England before Queen Elizabeth, and later she met the Queen and her husband, Prince Philip. That must have been quite an experience for the girl from Sevierville, Tennessee, who as a child had dreamed about being a princess.

In the United States, Parton was booked into leading rock concert halls. She attracted large crowds and received excellent reviews. Among the cities she played was New York, where she was applauded by celebrities such as Mick Jagger, Lily Tomlin, Candace Bergen, Andy Warhol, Bruce Springsteen, Phoebe Snow, Olivia Newton-John, and Terry Southern.

On stage Dolly still appears in a rhinestone-studded gown or tight-fitting pant-suit with heavy makeup on her face, a massive blond wig on her head, and flashing rings on her fingers. Her fingernails look like miniature swords, and she totters along on spike-heeled shoes. (Dolly is only 5 feet tall, "but I'm 6 feet 4 in heels," she jokes.) Her total appearance is as exaggerated as that of a child trying to dress up.

This is a "gimmick" for Parton, who underneath all the makeup is a truly beautiful woman. It is obvious that she is having fun and is deliberately overdressing. "I don't look this way out of ignorance," she would say. "If people think that I do, they're dumber than they think I am."

Most people have "gone along" with her appearance, which was once described as being "as delicious as an ice cream cone." Children are fascinated by Dolly. Adults admire her independence and her beauty. And fans of all ages are charmed by her singing. Only a Dolly Parton can make people

forget how she is dressed when she slips into her
little girl's voice for a tearful moment in a song
such as "Me and Little Andy." Many of Parton's
lyrics are "corny," but somehow she has been able
to cast a spell over the most cynical reviewers and
critics.

Once, when she was in New York City, she gave a free noon concert on the steps of city hall. Afterward, she was presented with the "Key to the City" by Mayor Edward Koch, and she answered questions from the audience of 5,000 in a spur-of-the-moment "people's press conference." It was an unusual and remarkably successful promotion for Dolly and her new "Heartbreaker" album.

Despite her continuing significant progress, a question lingers about Dolly Parton's future. Both her rooters and her critics wonder whether she will have the "staying power"—the continuing popularity—as a crossover performer that she had as a country music star.

Country music fans are noted for their loyalty. They consistently buy records by their favorite singers even when the records vary in quality. They support their favorites by attending concerts by an artist who has not had a hit for a long time. No such loyalty exists in the pop or rock fields, generally speaking. There is a saying in those fields that "you're only as good as your last song."

When Dolly was strictly a country singer she had a natural, down-to-earth quality that is a basic part of country music. She signed autographs for hours, ate with members of her band at a roadside diner, and made herself available for interviews. Doing these kinds of things makes for continuing loyalty in the country music business.

Dolly Parton—"as delicious as an ice cream cone"

Dolly says that she will not change in her new role. But change is unavoidable. It has been said that she wants to be "the female Elvis Presley of the entertainment world." If so, there is no way that people can approach her as they once did.

No one is more aware than Parton of the potential problems she faces. But Dolly has never feared what lies ahead. Instead, she sees the future as something to challenge her ambition and determination. "When I sit back in my rocking chair some day," she said, "I want to be able to say that I've done it all."

And if she does not do it all, it won't be because she didn't try. For Dolly Parton, trying has always been what life is all about.

Recordings of Dolly Parton

This list is limited to Dolly Parton albums that are available in most record stores. The albums include a wide selection of the artist's most representative work.

RECORD	LABEL	RECORD NO.
All I Can Do	RCA	AHL1-1665
Bargain Store	RCA	AHL1-0950
Best of Dolly Parton	RCA	AHL1-1117
Coat of Many Colors	RCA	AHL1-4603
Dolly	RCA	AHL1-1221
Dolly, Dolly, Dolly	RCA	AHL1-3546
Great Balls of Fire	RCA	AHL1-3361
Here You Come Again	RCA	AHL1-2544
I Wish I Felt This Way At Home	Camden	ACL-7002
In Concert	RCA	CPL2-1014
In the Beginning	Monument	MG-17623
Jolene	RCA	AHL1-0473
Just the Way I Am	Camden	2583
Love Is Like a Butterfly	RCA	AHL1-0712
Mine	Camden	ACL1-0307
My Tennessee Mountain Home	RCA	AHL1-0033
New Harvest . . . First Gathering	RCA	AHL1-2188

Index